Rebuilding Trust
after
Betrayal

Hope and Help for
Broken Relationships

GREGORY L. JANTZ, PHD

WITH KEITH WALL

AspirePress

Rebuilding Trust After Betrayal:
Hope and Help for Broken Relationships
© 2021 Gregory L. Jantz
Published by Aspire Press
An imprint of Tyndale House Ministries
Carol Stream, Illinois
www.hendricksonrose.com

ISBN 978-162862-989-7

Printed in the United States of America
010721VP

Contents

Amid Crisis, Cling *to* Hope

No matter how much hurt you are enduring and no matter how heartbroken you feel, there is hope.

You can cling to hope that you will not only *survive*, but will go on to *thrive*.

That is the message woven throughout these pages. My encouragement to cling to hope is not a pipe dream or a pep talk. It is a real-life conviction based on my thirty years of working as a mental-health professional treating a wide variety of serious issues, including addiction, depression, anxiety, eating disorders, trauma, and relationship problems.

Along the way, I have encountered countless instances of betrayal, where one person broke the trust of another and severely tested the limits that a close relationship can withstand when loyalty is compromised. When an act of dishonesty or disloyalty occurs, the relationship of those affected is turned upside down, shaken to the core.

In fact, when I discuss the topic of betrayal, I often use the metaphor of an earthquake rocking a person's world. Just like an actual earthquake, betrayal usually surfaces suddenly and dramatically, jolting you into a state of high anxiety and deep distress. The convulsion can bring numerous aftershocks that continue to rumble long after the initial impact.

When we use the word *betrayal*, our minds usually think first about infidelity within a marriage or other romantic relationship. This is indeed a devastating form of betrayal and is the primary focus in this book, but that certainly is not the only kind of disloyalty. Betrayal can also include:

- A close friend who undermines your relationship with lies, gossip, or manipulation.

- An addicted person who continually deceives family members and friends to support the compulsive behavior.

- A business or ministry associate whose misconduct jeopardizes the organization and leaves colleagues and partners in shock.

- A person in authority who violates the trust of someone under his or her care.

- A family member who steals from or swindles parents, siblings, or other related individuals.

These and other heart-rending incidents cause you to feel deeply shaken, if not completely shattered. I agree with psychologist Steven Stosny who says:

> Intimate betrayal strikes at the core of our capacity to trust and love, violating the fundamental

expectation that gives us the courage to connect deeply—the belief that the person we love won't intentionally hurt us. Whether the betrayal is through infidelity, emotional abuse, verbal aggression, or domestic violence, the psychological wound that cuts deepest is the perception that, ultimately, the person we love doesn't care about our well-being. When humans feel betrayed, we tend to withdraw from contact or furiously lash out in distress, just as do other mammals suffering intense pain.[1]

As I have worked with people crestfallen by an act of betrayal, I have been reminded of three essential points:

1. Betrayal, especially from someone close, is one of the most devastating experiences a person can endure.

There is simply no sugarcoating it—betrayal cuts to the core and hurts deeply. Usually, the closer the betrayer is to you, the more profound the hurt will be. Working through betrayal and repairing the damage will be one of the hardest things you'll do in life. It will take courage, perseverance, resilience, inner strength, and clear thinking.

2. Hope is a powerful ally in the quest to work through heartache and restore a damaged relationship.

Other factors are also essential to achieve healing, such as wise counsel, difficult conversations, support from friends, and maintaining boundaries. But I believe that hope is the indispensable quality that allows you to overcome doubts and press forward to a bright future.

GOD PROVIDES THE STRENGTH, GUIDANCE, AND PEACE TO OVERCOME YOUR CURRENT HEARTACHE AND REGAIN JOY.

3. God is the ultimate restorer, healer, and rebuilder of broken dreams.

As a person of faith, I am convinced that God wants each person to be fulfilled, enjoy rewarding relationships, and grow into their full potential. Broken relationships and dashed dreams will plummet you to the depths of despair—but

you don't need to stay there forever. God provides the strength, guidance, and peace to overcome your current heartache and regain joy. As Scripture assures us, "The God of all grace, who called you to his eternal glory in Christ, after you have suffered a little while, will himself restore you and make you strong, firm and steadfast" (1 Peter 5:10).

A Word *of* Caution

Please notice what I have *not* said: I have not promised your broken relationship *will* be repaired. Not all situations warrant the rebuilding of trust. This book will help you evaluate which category your relationship belongs in, as well as giving you the tools to heal.

In the pages ahead, we'll take a hard look at a hard topic. We'll explore how betrayal shakes the foundation of your relationship and perhaps your entire life. More important, we'll discuss how you can begin to pick up the pieces and move toward healing.

Amid crisis, choosing hope will sustain you and strengthen you for the journey to come. I encourage you to hold on to the slightest amount of hope you possess. In time, you will find that the smallest seed of hope can blossom into confidence, optimism, and faith.

CHAPTER ONE

The Earthquake of Betrayal

On Saturday morning, Kaylee poured herself a cup of coffee and settled into one of the chairs on the back deck. She wanted to enjoy a few moments of calm before her husband and six-year-old son returned from their walk to the park a few blocks away. It was a favorite Saturday morning ritual for Rob and Tyler—and Kaylee too, since it gave her a little time to herself.

Kaylee's phone vibrated with an incoming text. She picked up the phone, tapped on the picture, and laughed. Rob had just sent a goofy selfie of himself and Tyler on one of the playground slides.

Kaylee tapped on another notification, this one from Facebook messenger. As soon as she saw the name in her inbox, she was intrigued.

Why was Elizabeth messaging her? What in the world could her husband's ex-girlfriend have to say to her after all these years?

Rob and Elizabeth had dated in college for several years before going through a messy breakup. He had met Kaylee a few months later.

But all that was old news. Rob and Kaylee had just celebrated their twelfth wedding anniversary and were expecting a second baby in four months. Kaylee hadn't thought of Elizabeth in years, and Rob probably hadn't either.

So why was Elizabeth messaging her?

She tapped to find out.

Elizabeth's message was short and to the point.

As Kaylee read the three brief sentences, she felt time stand still as the world shifted around her. She closed her eyes and fought a sense of nausea as her life rocked out of control.

After what seemed like an eternity, the spinning sensation stopped. She realized she was holding her breath and told herself to breathe. She opened her eyes and gazed out on a life that looked and felt completely different than it had just a few moments earlier.

Every landmark was gone or moved.

Love. Trust. Security.

She couldn't get her bearings.

Her once lovely, predictable world lay in ruins around her.

She dropped her phone. As it hit the wood deck, the screen went black. But it didn't matter. The message was burned into her memory: "I want you to know that Rob and I are seeing each other again. I still love him and believe we never should have broken up, and I think he feels the same way. I didn't want this to come as a shock to you later, so I wanted to give you time to prepare."

Shaken Emotions *in the* Wake *of* Betrayal

Discovering that you've been betrayed by someone you trusted can feel like an earthquake registering the highest point on the Richter scale, rocking your world and turning the wonderful life you've built together into shambles. Or perhaps you feel that nothing was turned into shambles (besides your heart), because your perceived wonderful life was a sham from the beginning. And now you're simply seeing it for what it was all along.

Even when the initial shock of betrayal has passed, the aftershocks are endless. You have more questions than answers. Every day can bring new devastation as your brain works overtime trying to make sense of the rubble around you. Suddenly you remember small things—like your spouse's late nights at the office or the sound of frequent text notifications—that now take on new and painful meaning.

Plus your emotions are as jumbled as your world. You feel deeply confused and conflicted. Every new thought or revelation evokes a different shade of emotion. No wonder your feelings are all over the map.

You think ...

- "How could he do this to me?"

- "This can't be happening, can it?"

- "How could I have not seen this coming? I'm so stupid."

- "I must have caused this somehow. This must be my fault."

- "I can't deal with this now. I'll think about it tomorrow."

- "I'm so ashamed this happened. I don't want anyone to know."

- "This didn't happen. It's all a misunderstanding somehow."

- "My life is ruined forever. I'll never trust anyone again."

- "If I could hurt her as much as I'm hurting right now, that would feel fair and justified."

You feel ...

- **Angry**—at yourself, the person who deceived you, and other people involved.

- **Confused**—struggling to process what has happened.

- **Disoriented**—losing track of time and obligations.

- **Depressed**—feeling sad, hopeless, or numb.

- **Despair**—wondering how you're going to move on.

- **Jealous**—of the person, thing, or activity that seems to be valued over you.

- **Depleted**—sleep deprived, anxious, disruption in normal routine.

- **Ashamed**—believing you were foolish to be duped and offering trust that wasn't warranted.

- **Traumatized**—feeling intensely shaken, fearful, and anxious.

You may recognize in the list of common emotions some of the stages of grief—and for good reason. As we'll discuss more fully in Chapter Two, betrayal is indeed the loss of something profoundly precious, and those who have been betrayed may find themselves deeply grieving what they have lost.

Your emotions in the wake of betrayal are extremely intense, confusing, and jarring. This is to be expected as you begin the process of sorting through the debris and figuring out how to rebuild your heart and your life.

The Foundation of Healthy Relationships

If there were a recipe for a healthy, vibrant relationship, *trust* and *respect* would be the two key ingredients. These qualities lay the foundation for everything else that is positive and prosperous. Two people can enjoy great chemistry, similar work ethics, compatible goals and dreams. They can have great conversational skills and enjoy the same hobbies and recreational activities. But if trust and respect are missing—opening the door to distrust and disrespect—true intimacy will never be grasped, and the relationship will never thrive.

When you have trust, you enjoy powerful relationship attributes, including:

- **Reliability**—knowing that your loved one will be there for you and come through for you.

- **Fidelity**—knowing that your loved one will be loyal to you.

- **Peace of mind**—knowing there is no need to check on the person's whereabouts or wonder if you're being told the truth.

- **Emotional intimacy**—knowing that you don't have to stay guarded because your spouse has your best interests at heart.

■ **Authentic sexual intimacy**—knowing that you are not in the quandary of surrendering your body while guarding your heart, a combination that isn't healthy for anyone.

Likewise, when two people respect each other, it paves the way for dynamics such as kindness, patience, forgiveness, and understanding. Disrespect, on the other hand, creates a cacophony of discord. Belittling comments and eye rolls are just the beginning. We don't cooperate with people we don't respect, consider their needs and desires, help them realize their goals and potential, and we certainly don't stay in love with them.

BETRAYAL IS CATACLYSMIC BECAUSE IT SHATTERS BOTH TRUST AND RESPECT.

With this in mind, it's important to realize that trust can be broken by a single act of betrayal. And respect can be undermined by a single dramatic, disappointing action— or a thousand tiny slights. Betrayal is cataclysmic because it shatters *both* trust and respect. When these foundations are leveled, everything they supported—kindness, peace of mind, emotional and sexual intimacy, patience, understanding, and more—can crumble as well.

It's not surprising that when betrayal has rocked the foundation of two people, the future of that relationship feels uncertain. Can the relationship be saved? That may not be easily determined until this far more foundational question can be answered: *Can trust and respect be rebuilt?*

The Many Faces *of* Betrayal

Craig was ashamed to admit that sometimes he stood around the corner of his wife's home office and eavesdropped on her phone conversations with Jason, one of her clients.

Craig had never thought of himself as a jealous guy. But when Mary was on the phone with Jason, there was something about her intimate tone of voice, the way she laughed—and the personal things she shared—that turned Craig's heart inside out and caused his blood pressure to skyrocket.

One night at dinner, Craig tried to sound casual as he broached the topic with Mary. "So, you've been on the phone a lot with Jason."

Mary, a website designer, shrugged. "He's a client, Craig. We've been working on a project."

"Didn't his website launch a couple months ago?" Craig pressed.

That conversation sparked others over the coming weeks, and eventually Mary admitted that she had developed feelings for Jason. Nevertheless, the relationship had never turned physical, nor had she wanted it to. She loved Craig and didn't want to hurt their relationship by having an affair. She terminated the working arrangement with Jason and apologized to Craig for crossing emotional boundaries with another man.

Craig was relieved. At the same time, he couldn't get over how betrayed he felt: "It's not like she actually cheated on me," he told himself. "They talked too much on the phone. Big deal. So why do I feel so hurt and angry?"

As I have pointed out, betrayal is most often thought of as sexual infidelity, but betrayal can occur in numerous ways. Sometimes betrayal is sudden and traumatic; other times it is subtle and insidious. Mary's emotional affair with Jason is a prime example. Despite the fact that Mary hadn't experienced sexual intimacy with Jason, they had shared the kind of emotional intimacy couples reserve for each other—not for work clients. Her betrayal of Craig was real. No wonder he felt hurt and angry.

Financial infidelity is another example. This type of betrayal takes place when one person deceives a spouse about spending and debt. This can include a variety of financial activities done dishonestly, such as disregarding agreed-upon use of money, using credit cards secretively, reckless spending of money, or running up debt.

One woman who discovered that her husband had a secret financial life—complete with hidden accounts, spending habits, and debt—described her devastating feelings like this: "I felt everything about us as a couple had been a lie. The out-of-control spending and debt are very troubling, but sneakiness and secrecy are even worse."

SOMETIMES BETRAYAL IS SUDDEN AND TRAUMATIC; OTHER TIMES IT IS SUBTLE AND INSIDIOUS.

Addiction is another example of a serious betrayal. Susan lived for years with her husband's addiction to alcohol. Each time she found an empty bottle buried in the trashcan or detected the undeniable smell on Scott's breath, she felt deceived all over again. Scott had promised

numerous times to stop and to seek help for his problem. But Susan continually found evidence of his drinking— and no evidence that he was making a meaningful effort to change. "As much as I hate his drinking problem, I hate the lying most of all," she said. "I can't trust anything he says anymore. And I've lost respect for him too."

She says she still loves Scott, but some days she thinks about moving into her own place.

Susan continued: "I live in a state of hypervigilance, questioning everything he says, wondering constantly if he's been drinking, and checking my purse every day for missing cash. It's exhausting! And then sometimes I tell myself that it's no big deal. Scott is a good person in many ways. Maybe I'm over-reacting. And then I discover he's lied to me *again,* and I'm devastated all over again."

Sometimes one form of betrayal leads to another. For example, when Roger's wife became addicted to painkillers, she not only deceived her husband about her drug use, but she also stole drugs from the medicine cabinets of family members. And eventually, she began secretly emptying the couple's financial accounts to support her dependency. The betrayal of her addiction, with all of its deception, was compounded by financial infidelity that took the couple to the brink of bankruptcy.

People who have been betrayed in ways that don't involve sexual infidelity can find themselves questioning the validity of their feelings. After all, it's not like they found motel receipts for clandestine meet-ups. Yet betrayal in any form is devastating because it demolishes the very foundation of a healthy relationship.

We've mentioned emotional affairs, financial infidelity, and addictions. Here are some other forms that betrayal can take:

- Gambling

- Abuse (emotional, physical, spiritual)

- Social media misuse (choosing online "friends" and activities over one's real-life relationships)

- Persistent lying and deception

- Chronic use of pornography

The real betrayal, after all, is rooted in the disregard and disrespect shown by the disloyal party. In other words, the defining factor is deception—hidden choices that destroy trust and respect, and leave a relationship on shaky ground.

Why People Betray Others

It makes sense that the first question you feel desperate to have answered is "Why?"

- "Why in the world would you do this?"

- "Why have you risked everything we've created together for *this?*"

- "Why have you lied to me?"

It's understandable that questions like these are foremost in your mind, but be prepared that the answers may be slow to come—or may never come at all. It's possible that the person who betrayed you isn't in touch with all the "whys" driving his or her harmful choices. It's also possible they know the reason, but are not ready to put it into words. Or perhaps there are many reasons, leaving the person who broke your trust unwilling or unable to offer you more than an unsatisfactory, "It's complicated."

You may or may not ever discover the true reasons someone betrayed your love and trust, but it can be helpful to understand some of the factors that play a role in the choice to betray a loved one. Let me add that while factors like these may contribute to the choices someone makes, I am not suggesting that these factors justify those choices. Unmet needs, childhood trauma—even psychological disorders—are powerful dynamics and deserve to be addressed. Betraying a loved one, however, is never the right way to address even valid challenges.

Now let's take a look at some of these factors.

Unmet Emotional or Sexual Needs

When legitimate needs are met in illegitimate ways, the results can be devastating for everyone involved. If unmet needs contributed to the actions of your spouse, this is not to say that you bear responsibility for the choices he or she made. Even if a committed relationship is experiencing struggles or a season of disconnect, the right course of action is to be intentional about pursuing healing for the relationship—not pursuing comfort in the arms of someone new.

Lack of Commitment to Integrity

Let's face it—some people simply don't put a lot of stock in values such as integrity, honesty, and fidelity. There are myriad reasons this can occur, including personality disorders, poor role models as a child, or an education that did not emphasize honesty. But whatever the cause, someone who does not value honesty and integrity will have few internal compasses leading them away from temptation.

Unhealed Wounds from Childhood

Childhood trauma, if not addressed, can create a level of ongoing pain that leads to unhealthy coping mechanisms. Again, this does not justify or excuse the choice to betray a loved one, but it can help explain the driving force behind these kinds of destructive choices. If someone is dealing with the pain of childhood trauma, the best course of action is to be intentional about pursuing inner healing, not to self-medicate through dangerous living.

Sacrificing Long-term Fulfillment for Short-term Rewards

It takes maturity to understand the benefits of delaying gratification. It's also a skill that can be developed. Some people have never learned the value of sacrificing a small reward today in exchange for something of far greater value in the future.

You might be familiar with the landmark "marshmallow study." In the early 1960s, psychologist Walter Mischel conducted a study of preschoolers. In his experiment, children were given the choice of eating one marshmallow now, or two marshmallows in twenty minutes—if, of course, they could sit in a room and ignore marshmallow number one for that long.

Three decades later, Mischel and his associates followed up with the preschoolers, by then adults. They discovered that the children who were willing to delay gratification generally went on to achieve higher grades, better health, and greater overall success in life than the children who consumed the first marshmallow and chose not to delay gratification for a bigger reward later on.

People who have never grasped and practiced the art of delayed gratification will find it harder to say no to temporary pleasure, even if it means sacrificing a greater long-time good with someone they love.

SHAME IS ONE OF THE MOST POWERFUL EMOTIONS HUMANS FEEL, AND IT DRIVES PEOPLE TO DESTRUCTIVE BEHAVIORS.

Shame

I have come to believe that shame is one of the most powerful emotions humans feel, and it drives people to destructive behaviors. When we feel shame for any reason, it can fuel a spectrum of harmful actions and attitudes. Shame undermines the way we see ourselves, the way we think others view us, and the kind of future we want to pursue. If we are living with shame, we may find ourselves in danger of sabotaging even the good things in our lives—like a healthy relationship with someone we care about—especially if the resulting destruction confirms what shame has led us to believe about ourselves after all.

Personality Disorders

Narcissism, borderline disorder, and other mental health issues are often linked with chronic lying. Compulsive liars deceive others even when there is no reason to do so. They also lie without effort. In fact, lying may feel more natural to them then telling the truth. Some experts believe personality disorders can result from childhood trauma, low self-esteem, or anxiety.

Personality disorders and compulsive lying are deeply rooted and are difficult (if not impossible) behaviors to change. If you determine that you have been betrayed by a pathological liar or someone with a personality disorder, talk to a professional counselor about the chances for true contrition or change in your loved one. These conversations may help you as you process the possibility of rebuilding your relationship.

Impulse Control Deficit

The brain's prefrontal lobe is responsible for attention, decision-making, and impulse control. Conditions like ADHD and bipolar disorder can impact the performance of the prefrontal lobe, which can in turn weaken impulse control. There are also officially recognized impulse control disorders including pathological gambling and kleptomania.

Other factors—such as alcohol misuse—can also impair judgment and impulse control. There are effective ways to address impulse control disorders and, of course, sobriety is a helpful step for those with a history of alcohol-use problems.

Let me tell you about Charles and Emily. Thirty years ago, Charles was stationed overseas when he attended a party, drank too much, and woke up in bed with a woman who was not his wife. He told his wife, Emily, what had happened, and the event was pivotal in his decision to give up alcohol altogether.

Passive Aggressive Retaliation

Sometimes people engage in affairs or other deceptive behaviors as a way of getting back at a partner for something they did recently or even long ago. Eleven years after Charles cheated on Emily, she had a month-long affair with a coworker. She eventually told Charles about the relationship, adding, "Now the scales are balanced."

Sometimes the retaliation can seem unrelated. Someone can run up secret "debt" as a way of getting back at a spouse for an affair or have an emotional affair to get back at a spouse for cheating on the marriage with pornography.

You're Not Alone

Betrayal takes a heavy toll. What I want to stress to you is the importance of not going through this crisis alone. We'll discuss many practical survival strategies in Chapter Three, but for now, carefully consider who you can turn to for support as you begin to process your shock over the betrayal.

Professional counseling, wise friends, and church communities are places you may want to consider. One word of caution: We all have friends who may have been betrayed themselves at some point and would immediately

"LET US THEN APPROACH GOD'S THRONE OF GRACE WITH CONFIDENCE, SO THAT WE MAY RECEIVE MERCY AND FIND GRACE TO HELP US IN OUR TIME OF NEED."

—Hebrews 4:16

encourage us to leave any relationship with someone who was disloyal.

I am not telling you that every broken relationship must or should be saved—or that your relationship should be scrapped or restored. But seeking counsel from friends whose advice to you is based on their own pain—rather than on what's possible or best for you—doesn't give you the chance to find out. As you consider who to include in your inner circle of support, look for people who have a healthy, untainted perspective that will allow them to help you find the right path of healing for you. And don't hesitate to ask God for help. He is, after all, the ultimate ally, and able to bring people into your life who can help carry you through.

THE HONEST TRUTH ABOUT DISHONEST PEOPLE

What is your tolerance for people who deceive you? Maybe you're reluctantly willing to put up with the occasional "little white lie."

YOU DESERVE TO BE TREATED WITH DIGNITY, HONOR, AND INTEGRITY.

Or maybe you have a zero-tolerance policy. Whatever your personal standards about dishonesty and deception, it's important to know that lies don't come out of nowhere. That is, people who tell them have underlying issues that lead them to deceive. These include:

Dishonest people have a poorly developed conscience.

A person's conscience is the internal guidance system that leads him or her to do the right thing, behave humanely, and treat others with compassion. In contrast, dishonest people act out of their own desires and impulses, paying little attention to how their actions might affect you. If they can get their own way, even if that causes you pain, they will do so.

Dishonest people are often deceitful as a way of life.

People willing to deceive in one situation or with one person will find it easy to deceive in other contexts. A person who manipulates a coworker may manipulate you. If a person "shades the truth" with his boss or pads her expense report, he or she will be inclined to be dishonest with you as well.

Dishonest people do not know how to develop trust—or don't value it.

Lies destroy a crucial component of any relationship: trust. Honesty is the essential ingredient for trust, and without it, a relationship will be on shaky ground. People who lie either do not care about maintaining trust with you or do not understand how important it is for long-term stability.

Dishonest people don't respect others.

Respect between two people ensures proper conduct and communication in many ways. You don't want to do anything that would jeopardize someone you hold in high esteem. But lack of respect leads to all kinds of relational troubles, including manipulation, dishonesty, and cheating.

Dishonest people lack courage.

Oftentimes, it's hard to tell the truth and much easier to cover over awkward situations with a lie. Being honest frequently means taking personal responsibility, risking conflict with someone, and admitting failure—all of which require courage. Instead of admitting their shortcomings and addressing tough issues, dishonest people take the easy way out.

Dishonest people love themselves more than others (including you).

People deceive to gain some advantage, impress others, or get what they want. Their life motto is, "It's all about me!" Dishonest people don't consider how others will be affected or care what the consequences will be.

This whole discussion boils down to one emphatic point: You deserve to be treated with dignity, honor, and integrity. This isn't to say that someone who betrayed you can't change. People certainly do grow and develop. Still, knowing these characteristics of dishonest people will help you evaluate if consistent change is indeed possible. You deserve nothing less than that.

The apostle Paul wrote to believers in Corinth:

"WE ARE GLAD WHENEVER WE ARE WEAK BUT YOU ARE STRONG; AND OUR PRAYER IS THAT YOU MAY BE FULLY RESTORED. THIS IS WHY I WRITE THESE THINGS WHEN I AM ABSENT, THAT WHEN I COME I MAY NOT HAVE TO BE HARSH IN MY USE OF AUTHORITY—THE AUTHORITY THE LORD GAVE ME FOR BUILDING YOU UP, NOT FOR TEARING YOU DOWN. FINALLY, BROTHERS AND SISTERS, REJOICE! STRIVE FOR FULL RESTORATION, ENCOURAGE ONE ANOTHER, BE OF ONE MIND, LIVE IN PEACE. AND THE GOD OF LOVE AND PEACE WILL BE WITH YOU."

—2 Corinthians 13:9-11

CHAPTER TWO

The Shockwaves *of* Betrayal

When you have experienced the earthquake of betrayal, the shockwaves reverberate throughout your life. Betrayal is a form of trauma, and trauma is never compartmentalized, confined to just one distinct part. Trauma spills out in all directions. In the weeks and months after betrayal has come to light, you might experience sleep disruption, depression or anxiety, persistently troubling thoughts, diminished work productivity, and low motivation.

I say all of this not to make you feel even worse, but to assure you that your feelings are normal and natural. You have suffered a major jolt to your life, and it takes considerable time, courage, and effort before the aftershocks begin to subside. Healing happens at its own pace, in its own way, and can't be hurried.

Over the past three decades, I have worked with scores of individuals who have suffered a betrayal of one kind or another. And I have observed that betrayal often parallels the stages of grief. That is because betrayal brings with it significant losses, including the loss of stability, the loss of trust, the loss of inner peace, and the loss of dreams.

The stages of grief were developed by the Swiss-American psychiatrist Elizabeth Kübler-Ross in her 1969 book, *On Death and Dying*. While her principles were originally devised for terminally ill people, these stages of grief have been adapted for other experiences with loss, including betrayal.

Everyone grieves differently, but there are some commonalities in the stages experienced during betrayal.

5 STAGES OF GRIEF

ANGER   DEPRESSION

DENIAL   BARGAINING   ACCEPTANCE

Stage 1: Denial

In this stage, the betrayed person might think:

- "I don't believe it!"

- "No way he/she could do this to me."

- "There must be some mistake."

It's not unusual to respond to intense sudden feelings by initially pretending the event didn't happen. Denying the traumatic revelation gives you time to gradually absorb the news and begin to process it. This is a common defense mechanism and helps numb you to the intensity of the situation. Denial helps you to, for a time, minimize the deep pain you suddenly feel.

As you move out of the denial stage, however, the emotions you've been hiding will begin to rise. You'll be confronted with a lot of anger and sorrow you have suppressed.

Another word about this first phase: Sometimes, when there has been a history of mistrust and broken promises within the relationship, the betrayed person sidesteps denial and goes straight to shock, acknowledging what happened and feeling devastated by it. In fact, you can believe the deceitful person has mistreated you, but the seismic waves leave you staggering and reeling.

Stage 2: Anger

Here, the response is obvious and expected:

- ▪ "I feel infuriated!"

- ▪ "How could you do this to me? To us?"

- ▪ "I have every right to be mad!"

Anger is a normal and justified response to betrayal because of the deception, injustice, and disrespect involved. It does no good to pretend you're not angry or to minimize the emotions. Progress comes from looking honestly at your strong feelings and working through them.

There is so much to process that anger usually becomes a prominent emotion. Anger tends to be the first thing we feel when we start to release emotions related to betrayal. These painful feelings and the tendency to either lash out or withdraw emotionally can make productive communication very difficult with the dishonest person.

Anger may mask itself in feelings like bitterness or resentment. It may not be clear-cut fury or rage. As the anger subsides, however, you may begin to think more rationally about what's happening and feel the emotions you've been pushing aside.

Stage 3: Bargaining

You might find yourself thinking:

- "If only I had been more attentive and aware, this wouldn't have happened."

- "If I had been a better spouse, he wouldn't have cheated."

- "We'll just act like this never happened if you promise not to do it again."

Grief counselors sometimes use the word *bargaining* to describe this process of envisioning an alternate reality in which your loss did not occur. Given the intense emotions following betrayal, it's not uncommon to look for ways to regain control or to want to feel like you can control the outcome of an event.

PROGRESS COMES FROM LOOKING HONESTLY AT YOUR STRONG FEELINGS AND WORKING THROUGH THEM.

Bargaining is a line of defense against overwhelming emotions. It helps you postpone sadness, confusion, or hurt. We also tend to make the assumption that if things had played out differently, we would not be in such an emotionally painful place in our lives.

Stage 4: Depression

At this stage, you might think:

- "I feel so down about this situation."

- "I don't think I'll ever recover from this blow."

- "I can't go on."

Like the other stages of grief, depression can be overwhelming. You may feel lethargic, gloomy, and confused. In those moments, we tend to pull inward as the sense of depression deepens. We might find ourselves retreating, being less sociable, and reaching out less to others about what we are going through. Some experts call depression "anger turned inward," and that may be the case following betrayal—especially if anger is not properly worked through. In the early stages following an act of betrayal, you may be running from the emotions, trying to stay a step ahead of them. By this stage, however, you may be able to confront them and begin to address them.

THERE ARE STILL MANY BAD DAYS, BUT THE GOOD DAYS WILL BECOME MORE AND MORE FREQUENT.

Stage 5: Acceptance

At this stage, you can finally say:

- "This terrible thing happened, but it need not define us or ruin our relationship."

- "Though extremely painful, this betrayal can be worked through and overcome."

- "I feel wounded, but I can survive this."

Acceptance doesn't mean you've "moved on" or "gotten over" the betrayal. It does, however, mean that you have accepted it and have come to understand what it means in your life now. You've had a major upheaval in your life, and that changes the way you feel about many things. You can't expect things to "go back to the way they were," but you can expect to eventually regain joy and contentment. Look to acceptance as a way to see that there are still many bad days, but the good days will become more and more frequent.

When we come to a place of acceptance, it is not that we won't feel the pain involved, but rather that we are no longer resisting the reality of our situation and are purposefully looking for ways to heal and grow through the experience.

Can This Relationship Be Saved?

As you experience these stages of grief—either all of them or some of them—you will inevitably ask if you want to remain in and repair the damaged relationship. Or if it's wisest to end the relationship and move on.

While forgiveness after an offense is always advisable—letting go to free yourself from lingering bitterness and pain—resuming the relationship is not. Sometimes resetting the relationship is the right choice; sometimes it's not. The key to begin repairing the damage: making the decision to remain committed to the relationship and investing the hard work to improve it.

Depending upon the type and severity of the wrongdoing, the betrayed person may be justified in ending the relationship. In some cases, the best course of action might be to sever ties (in situations involving abuse, for example).

Here are six questions to help you know what's right for you.

1. Did the betrayal involve physical or psychological abuse?

If the answer is yes, to any degree, you absolutely must protect yourself (and others) from potential future harm. And you should seriously consider ending the relationship altogether. Threatening, manipulative, and abusive behavior is rarely an isolated event. Odds are good that abusive behavior will continue. (This is a complex topic, and I encourage you to read the book I wrote with my colleague Dr. Tim Clinton, *Don't Call It Love: Breaking the Cycle of Relationship Dependency*.)

2. Did the person take responsibility for his/her action or try to minimize it?

In many years of counseling people through crises involving betrayal, I've observed that taking responsibility is essential for rebuilding trust. Some people try to brush off the offense and pretend it was "no big deal." Others blame-shift, acting as if the behavior was someone else's fault. Failure to take full responsibility leaves the betrayed person questioning—for good reason—whether the other person is truly contrite and willing to change.

3. Has there been a pattern of deceptive behavior or was the betrayal an out-of-character event?

This only applies to infractions that don't rise to the level of abusive behavior. Rather, it's meant to help you consider that the mistake might very well be a one-time event. Sometimes people do foolish things and recognize them as such—and take responsibility. This does not diminish the impact on the betrayed person, but it should be factored in when deciding whether to continue with the relationship.

4. If the person has apologized, does it consist of more than words?

Is there tangible evidence that the person truly understands how the betrayal hurt you and is willing to alter his or her behavior? Rebuilding trust must be built on verifiable change, not just promises.

5. Is the damage so severe that your relationship will forever be hampered and burdened by the betrayal?

Everyone will have a different answer to this question depending on their beliefs, background, past woundedness, the health of the relationship previously, and the circumstances of the betrayal. It is important to be able to overcome a betrayal and not be held back in the future if you think this act will be an ongoing burden.

6. Can you ever truly trust this person again?

When you first learn of an act of betrayal, your first reaction will likely be, "I could never trust you again!" That is a justifiable response. But when anger subsides and you work through your emotions, you can better evaluate if regained trust is in fact possible or impossible.

Pursue Productive (Though Painful) Discussions

Your decision to begin rebuilding trust will inevitably involve numerous conversations, many of them painful. You will need to talk through the factors that led to the act of betrayal and, equally important, how you will go about rebuilding a relationship of hope, health, and wholeness. These discussions are often extremely difficult, laden with intense emotions and confusing thoughts.

REBUILDING TRUST MUST BE BUILT ON VERIFIABLE CHANGE, NOT JUST PROMISES.

To ensure positive, productive discussions, include the following strategies.

Have a Vision.

Borrow a trick from great athletes and visualize your desired outcome for a tough conversation before you even begin. This will help you focus your talk on a solution and ultimately manifest a positive result. It might even be helpful to share your vision and intention with the other person at the outset so they understand that you ultimately want to find a resolution.

Use "I" Statements.

One of the fastest ways to get people on the defensive in a conversation is to verbally point your finger by saying:

- "You always …"

- "You never …"

- "You should have known …"

Instead, try to frame all of your statements with the word "I." This allows the other person to understand that you are merely stating your perspective. Try to begin sentences with:

- "I feel …"

- "When I …"

- "My concern is …"

Ask Questions First.

Seek to truly understand the other person's perspective by asking thoughtful questions. If you don't understand what's being said or the motive behind the other person's perspective, ask for clarification. Sometimes it's helpful to restate what you heard the other person say to ensure that you interpreted their words correctly. After they finish speaking, follow up with, "What I hear you saying is …"

Listen Actively.

Just because your ears are open doesn't mean you are listening to what the other person is saying. Hone your listening skills by staying present, making eye contact, and not interrupting. Also, avoid getting distracted by planning your response or finding fault in what the other person is saying while they are still talking.

YOUR TONE IS ABOUT FIVE TIMES MORE IMPORTANT THAN WHAT YOU SAY.

Consider Your Tone.

Have you ever had someone tell you "I'm sorry," but knew they didn't mean it? Even though their words communicated an apology, their tone sounded defiant and unapologetic. This is because the actual words you use account for

only about 7 percent of how people interpret what you say, while tone counts for about 38 percent. That means your tone is about five times more important than what you say. So make sure you come across as genuine, regardless of what you have to say.

Be Aware *of* Body Language.

So what makes up the other 55 percent of communication? You guessed it: body language. Our brains are wired to pick up on even the slightest nuances in nonverbal signaling. Not only should you learn to read other people's body language, you should become aware of your own nonverbal communication as well.

Focus on the Behavior.

If you are delivering criticism, make sure to differentiate between criticism of a *person* and criticism of a *behavior.* Notice the difference between saying, "You are really negative," versus, "When you point out the flaws in other people, it makes me feel discouraged." Criticizing the person directly simply makes him or her defensive, whereas discussing the behavior gives the person an opportunity to change.

"THE RIGHTEOUS CRY OUT, AND THE LORD HEARS THEM; HE DELIVERS THEM FROM ALL THEIR TROUBLES. THE LORD IS CLOSE TO THE BROKENHEARTED AND SAVES THOSE WHO ARE CRUSHED IN SPIRIT."

—Psalm 34:17-18

Your Relationship *with* Yourself

Rebuilding trust centers on another key component: Your own emotional health and well-being.

How you feel about yourself affects all of your other relationships. You may not be familiar with the idea that you have a relationship with yourself, but you do. You have a personality and a will; you have a perspective on life that is lived out in how you think, speak, feel, and act. Every day you interact with yourself. You make judgments about yourself and see life from the prism of your own worldview.

You have a relationship with yourself, and how you view that relationship matters:

TO REBUILD A HEALTHY RELATIONSHIP WITH ANOTHER PERSON, YOU NEED A HEALTHY RELATIONSHIP WITH YOURSELF.

- If I understand this relationship with myself *positively*, I can acknowledge, appreciate, and accept this self: "I like myself, I forgive myself, and I understand myself."

- If I see myself *negatively*, the self is not a source of strength

49

and comfort but a source of fear and concern. I might even distance thoughts through the use of second person ("you"): "Why did you do that and how could you be so stupid?"

When the self is the enemy, each day is a battle with the self, trying to be with the self as little as possible, finding ways to distract and create distance from the self. When my relationship with myself is suspect, my relationships with others become suspect and have shaky foundations. The shakier those relationships are, the more time, energy, and effort need to be placed into shoring them up and repairing damage.

> "ARE NOT FIVE SPARROWS SOLD FOR TWO PENNIES? YET NOT ONE OF THEM IS FORGOTTEN BY GOD. INDEED, THE VERY HAIRS OF YOUR HEAD ARE ALL NUMBERED. DON'T BE AFRAID; YOU ARE WORTH MORE THAN MANY SPARROWS."
>
> —Luke 12:6-7

I'm sure you see my point: To rebuild a healthy relationship with another person, you need a healthy relationship with yourself. Your sense of self-worth, self-respect, and self-confidence matter tremendously when it comes to your own future and the future of your relationship. Mutual support and comfort are certainly among the gifts that two people bring to a healthy relationship. But that only pays off when you approach each other on a footing of personal autonomy and empowerment. You can't offer someone what you don't have.

WHERE DOES RESPONSIBILITY LIE?

In the aftermath of betrayal and in the effort to rebuild trust, one vital aspect to explore is whether your relationship has become intertwined, dependent, and enabling. If it has developed unhealthy patterns, you could be making it harder to heal by a destructive loss of your ability to set and hold boundaries.

Therapists originally coined the word *codependent* to describe someone in a relationship with an addict with a tendency to make unwise sacrifices to enable that person's dysfunction. These days, the term covers a much broader range of compensating behaviors that add up to losing your personal autonomy in search of security. Even if your actions are simply efforts to avoid abusive or hurtful treatment from another, carefully consider ways you may unintentionally be harming your relationship by accepting responsibility in the relationship that doesn't belong to you.

- Do I tend to look for the cause of the other person's unacceptable behavior in myself?

- Do I help the other person feel more comfortable with bad behavior instead of expecting him or her to make the effort to improve?

- Do I compensate for his or her flaws, even to the point of enabling self-destructive behavior?

- Do I need constant reassurance, and am I willing to do anything to get it, including sacrificing my own wants and needs?

If you've recognized unhealthy patterns, take heart. The good news is, you're not trapped! You can be free of the fears and habits that have limited you thus far. Above all, communicate. Be courageous. Be honest. Talk to each other about the problem.

Next, commit to addressing past pain that fans the flames of insecurity by seeking professional help, if necessary. The reasons for unhealthy relationship patterns may be rooted in your past experiences, but it's up to you whether you take them into your future.

CHAPTER THREE

Rebuilding *the* Foundation

When Gary and Rita got married, they agreed that owning a house of their own would be a high priority in their new partnership. Each looked forward to starting a family and wanted their future children to have a permanent place to call home. This was particularly important to Gary, since his father was an Air Force officer whose career demands required the family to move frequently. Gary was determined his kids would have something he never did—the chance to put down roots.

Gary and Rita both had rewarding jobs, but not very high-paying ones. That meant that to reach their goal of home ownership would require a level of frugality and sacrifice they had not experienced as single people. Still, they were excited and motivated by their dream.

Together they wrote a budget and made a plan to save every month toward a down payment. The strategy included carefully building and safeguarding their credit so they could qualify for a mortgage when the time was right. For two years Gary took extra shifts every chance he got, and their savings account slowly grew.

"It was hard," he said. "I struggled to resist the urge to buy something I wanted or eat out more often. But I did resist because I thought we were both making those sacrifices. Turned out, that wasn't true."

Just after their second anniversary, Rita came to Gary with a painful confession. A few months after the wedding, she had obtained a credit card that Gary knew nothing about. When she reached the modest limit on that card, Rita got another. And then another, each with a higher borrowing limit. So long as she made the minimum payments, credit card companies rewarded her with more.

By the time she approached Gary, the combined balance due on the cards was $28,000—and she could no longer keep up on her own, or keep hiding the fact from her husband.

"It started off as a kind of harmless relief valve," Rita said. "Or so I told myself. I just wasn't used to being so tight all the time. I really did believe in our goal, but I felt like I was suffocating without a treat now and then. The secret credit card allowed me to splurge a little without disappointing Gary."

Of course, that's not what happened. As he digested the news, Gary felt the ground shake beneath his feet and everything solid in his life seemed to crumble. He felt very disappointed, as well as hurt, angry, dismayed, and … *betrayed*. As is so often the case, the financial reality wasn't the hardest part; it was being lied to and deceived.

"Honestly, I wondered how we could go on as a couple after that," he said. "If you don't have trust anymore, then what do you have?"

The Burning Question

Once trust is gone, Gary wondered, what does the concept of "relationship" even mean?

That's the painful puzzle many people face who've suffered something similar—and what makes the message and the mission of this book so important to me. It's about helping people figure out how to move beyond the emotional impasse that Gary and Rita reached in the hope of finding a way to reconcile what's in danger of remaining fractured forever—all for lack of trust.

Granted, as we've discussed earlier, sometimes reconciliation—restoring normal relations with someone—is neither possible nor advisable. The magnitude of the betrayal or the threat of repeat offenses—such as in cases of physical, emotional, or sexual abuse—presents too wide a gulf to bridge. True reconciliation requires three essential elements to succeed:

- A sense of safety

- A belief that a genuine change of behavior is possible

- A desire to move forward into a shared future once more

Without those, trust is likely to be gone forever.

Often times, the offenses we commit against each other—no matter how painful and shocking they may seem at the time—do not meet the standard of irreparable harm. If everyone involved approaches the healing process in good faith and with committed resolve—that is, if the ones who transgressed and the ones who were betrayed all *want* to heal—then reconciliation and a new beginning are certainly possible.

True reconciliation requires:

1. A sense of safety.

2. A belief that a genuine change of behavior is possible.

3. A desire to move forward into a shared future once more.

However, many people I've counseled over the years mistakenly believe that desire is *all* they need. They want to restart their relationships quickly and easily, like they do a frozen smartphone. Or perhaps—fueled by Hollywood's simplistic version of reconciliation, generally wrapped up in one power-packed scene near the climax of a film—these people become dismayed and disappointed by the hard reality: there's nothing simple or easy about getting over betrayal. Like rebuilding a town after an earthquake, there's no getting around the fact that reconstruction happens one fallen brick at a time.

Yet the good news is that it's absolutely within reach. For those who have decided their broken relationships are worth salvaging—and who feel safe in making the attempt—the pages ahead present a blueprint to address the obvious question: "How?"

A Process, Not *a* Magic Pill

Below, I offer step-by-step answers to that "how?" question in three sections:

- What to do when someone has betrayed your trust

- What to do when you did the betraying

- What to do together

Before you dive in, however, be sure to digest these important facts:

Reconciliation takes two (or more).

You can't just work through the list that applies to you and ignore the things to be done together or expect to succeed if the other person or people involved are not engaged.

Reconciliation takes work.

There is no autopilot feature. Be prepared to show up every day to do your part, even when you don't feel like it.

Reconciliation takes a willingness to risk vulnerability and further pain.

As you proceed, you'll be called on to open yourself to desires and emotions—in yourself and others— that may have been previously hidden. This can be uncomfortable and trigger a "fight or flight" response. Make up your mind now to accept that in exchange for the chance to come out on the other side with relationships that might even be stronger than ever.

Reconciliation takes time.

If a car jumps the curb tonight and runs over your cherished rose bushes, you'll accept that they will not bounce back in a day. If you suffer a broken leg during a mountain-climbing expedition, you know the recovery process will take many months. There's no way around it: healing takes as long as it takes, so be patient.

What *to* Do When Someone Has Betrayed Your Trust

Here are ten steps that will bring you a little closer to restored trust every day.

STEP 1   Affirm Your Commitment.

Are you truly invested in the process or not? If you're in, then now is the time to seal off the exits and close all the escape hatches. Make a list of your "conditions" for participation—and then consciously set them aside. Anticipate your excuses for not following through and answer them in advance.

The point is, in choosing reconciliation over discord, you've taken a difficult road. It's critical to have your eyes wide open—and your resolve firmly established—from the very first step.

STEP 2 — Begin to Forgive.

I can almost hear the objections you might be voicing right now. I can sense your temptation to close the book and put it down (or throw it across the room). Believe me, I understand. How can this next step on the road to reconciliation be the one thing you think may never be possible?

Yet you need to begin this process for a very good reason because everything that follows depends upon getting this part right. Most of us react strongly to the idea that we must forgive a painful betrayal largely because *we don't understand it.* In a moment, I'll deal with that and share what I've learned about forgiveness. But before getting to the details of *what* it is and isn't, let's spend time talking about *why* forgiveness is so important.

The purpose here is to show you how to repair a relationship that has been broken by someone else's betrayal. Presumably, you've read this far because you want to do that and want to do it successfully. When I first met Gary, he was still extremely angry and hurt over what Rita had done to damage his dream of owning a home. But he said he had chosen to try and work through all that and save his marriage. He was committed, he told me. Whatever it takes.

Until I mentioned the word *forgiveness*.

"Oh no," he said. "I can never forgive her for this. We'll move on and put things back together, but that's too much to ask."

RECONCILIATION WITHOUT FORGIVENESS IS IMPOSSIBLE.

"Well, then, you're wasting your time right now," I said.

Why? Because here is the fact that all who find themselves in Gary's shoes must understand: Reconciliation without forgiveness is impossible.

Without forgiveness, life after a painful offense becomes a perpetual war zone. For your part, you are likely to remain on high alert for any new offense, while the one who betrayed you feels vulnerable to retaliation at a moment's notice and that they'll keep on paying the price forever. Under these conditions, a sort of "no man's land" develops between you—which is an effective way to kill a relationship, not to save one. The other eight steps in this section depend on openness, communication, vulnerability, honesty, safety, and the mutual attempt to put trust back on its feet. None of that can succeed if the air is still thick with judgment and recrimination.

With that in mind, it's worth spending time to dispel the confusion about the true nature of forgiveness that most people harbor. Let's start with what forgiveness is *not*.

Forgiveness is *not* about letting someone "off the hook."

The first and most powerful objection we encounter in ourselves when considering forgiveness is the mistaken idea that forgiveness means looking the other way while somebody "gets away" with something. We see forgiveness as an undeserved "get out of jail free" card. That seems wrong somehow, because we can't stand the idea of saying "It's okay" about behavior that clearly is not okay.

But forgiving someone does not mean their offense is okay. In fact, the purpose of forgiveness is not to deliver anything at all to the one who caused us harm, but to benefit *ourselves* by letting go of toxic attachment to the past and to our pain. So long as we hang on to feelings of outrage, injustice, and desire for payback, we keep the offense alive and the wounds fresh. And in the process, we remain vulnerable to all the negative physical and psychological effects of runaway anger and fear.

Think of it this way: Somebody makes a choice that causes you harm and pain. That person is not a monster, just a flawed human being like anyone else. Once the offense has occurred, there is no longer anything you can do about it. The offense happened. But from that moment forward, what comes next is your choice. Will you cling to the transgression, keeping it alive and even making matters worse for yourself? Or will you let go of the need for "justice" and for answers to vague and useless questions like "Why me?"

> "BEAR WITH EACH OTHER AND FORGIVE ONE ANOTHER IF ANY OF YOU HAS A GRIEVANCE AGAINST SOMEONE. FORGIVE AS THE LORD FORGAVE YOU."
>
> —Colossians 3:13

Forgiveness is the way you do this. Without making any excuses for the other person's bad behavior, and without shielding them from the consequences of their actions, you have the power to say, "I no longer hold this against you. I am moving on."

Forgiveness is *not* a sign of weakness or an invitation to further offense.

This fear is rooted in the ancient human impulse to take "an eye for an eye and a tooth for a tooth." In other words, in the belief that if we don't deal out retribution, we hold open the door for more trespasses of our boundaries.

And yet, ask yourself this: Which is a bigger sign of weakness, letting the offensive actions of someone else determine your future health and well-being; or taking charge of your own destiny by choosing forgiveness over bondage to anger and fantasies of revenge? You could make a show of "strength" by stoking your anger and outrage indefinitely, but that's just an illusion. You won't be weak by forgiving; just the opposite. As Chinese philosopher Lao Tzu wrote, "Mastering others is strength; mastering yourself is true power."

Forgiveness is *not* a feeling.

Many people think forgiveness has to be a warm and fuzzy emotional experience. That's what makes it seem so out of reach when you've suffered a painful betrayal. The very last thing you are capable of is conjuring up well-wishes and feelings of goodwill. Fortunately, you have to do no such thing.

Which brings us to what forgiveness *is*.

Forgiveness *is* a choice.

Plain and simple, forgiveness is a choice. It's a clear-eyed decision to cancel a debt, not solely for the benefit of the person who harmed you, but for your own future well-being. Forgiveness not only forecloses the negative physical, psychological, and emotional effects of harboring resentment, but it also opens the pathway to reconciliation. It makes possible the potential for having a stronger relationship than before, because you've both done what it took to work your way through the challenge of betrayal to life on the other side.

Forgiveness *is* in alignment with God's idea for how human beings can live together through thick and thin.

The apostle Paul wrote, "Be kind and compassionate to one another, forgiving each other, just as in Christ God forgave you" (Ephesians 4:32). Yes, the betrayal happened. No, you should not deny that or give up your right to set and hold boundaries. But if you want to put your life back together and grow past your pain, forgiveness is God's powerful plan for success.

FORGIVENESS IS GOD'S POWERFUL PLAN FOR SUCCESS.

Abandon Your Status as "Victim" and Consider Your Role in What Has Occurred.

It's possible that this step will come as an even bigger shock than the previous advice to forgive. "*My* role? I'm not the one on trial here," you might say. "I *am* the victim."

The way most people think, suffering a painful betrayal automatically places them on moral high ground, righteously aggrieved, and entitled to set the agenda. I'm not mocking those feelings; they are real and even justified.

But this brings us to another important milestone that's essential to your success in reconciling with the one who hurt you: *No one* is on trial. That's because you have chosen reconciliation, not recrimination; restoration, not revenge.

Initially, Gary could only see the damage that Rita's betrayal had caused, and what he had suffered as a result. He adopted the mantle of victim, certain that it was a perfect fit under the circumstances.

"Is it possible," I asked him, "that there is more to your desire to own a home than meets the eye? That the stakes are actually much higher than they appear?"

He thought for moment and then said, "What do you mean?"

"Maybe that you feel so strongly about it—even as if it's a matter of life and death—because of unresolved emotions you've carried about having to move so often as a child. What was that like?"

"It was terrible," Gary admitted.

"How did it affect your relationships?"

"I stopped making friends to avoid the pain of losing them in eighteen months," he said.

"So, for you, having a permanent place to call home is a way to finally put that pain to rest."

"For my kids, yes," he replied.

"And for you," I added.

Gary said nothing, but the truth of that was visible in his expression.

I continued to clarify: "Is it possible that Rita felt the emotional weight of that, and that it was too much for her to carry?"

Please notice that nothing in this idea suggests that Rita was *justified* in her actions. Nor does it seek to give Gary a portion of the blame. Done right, this kind of self-examination is an opportunity to let healing proceed on *multiple* fronts at once, strengthening the foundation for a better relationship going forward. It also serves as a reminder that the moral high ground is actually a slippery slope.

As Jesus said, "How can you say to your brother, 'Let me take the speck out of your eye,' when all the time there is a plank in your own eye? You hypocrite, first take the plank out of your own eye, and then you will see clearly to remove the speck from your brother's eye" (Matthew 7:4–5).

THE MORAL HIGH GROUND IS ACTUALLY A SLIPPERY SLOPE.

Betrayal never happens in a vacuum, but rather in a compli-cated, interwoven *context* of human desires, reasons, pressures, frailties, wounds, and flaws. A breakthrough Gary made in his process of rebuilding trust came when he realized that his single-minded need to save every penny was fueled

by personal pain, and that it may have been unfair to expect Rita, who lacked such a powerful motive, to mirror his capacity for sacrifice.

Make Necessary Course Corrections of Your Own.

Now that you've given up your special status as "victim"—in recognition that we are all just human—be sure to follow through with meaningful action. Through the process of examining how your own actions,

REBUILDING TRUST REQUIRES EVERYONE TO FEEL SAFE AND CONFIDENT THE PROCESS CAN SUCCEED.

attitudes, habits, beliefs, biases, and blind spots may have played a role in the painful betrayal you experienced, you'll likely discover areas you need to work on. When you identify a way you can improve yourself, then *do* it. In places that are prone to earthquakes, rigid building codes develop slowly. Each quake reveals another weakness in how things have been done, and wise leaders correct those things in anticipation of the next one.

This will clearly communicate that you are committed to making your *whole* relationship better, not just the parts the other person needs to work on. It is tangible proof that you really are in this together with the person who harmed you. That may seem backward at first. After all, it was the other person who committed

72

the betrayal, not you. (And in the next section I'll lay out the steps *that person* must take.)

But consider this: Rebuilding trust, as we've seen, requires *everyone* to feel safe and confident the process can succeed, not just you. As powerful as your fight-or-flight impulse is, the offender's is even more so because it is likely be fueled by feelings of guilt and shame as well. So anything you can do to offer assurance that they are not just being prepared for the gallows is helpful to your cause and theirs.

Far more important than that, however, is how you yourself will benefit when self-reflection leads to meaningful change, not just talk. Author Richard Bach wrote, "There is no such thing as a problem without a gift for you in its hands."[2] This step in your journey is about making sure you don't miss out on the gift.

We have all experienced a conversation in which the words coming out of someone's mouth obviously did not match what they really thought and felt. At worst, that can be a kind of passive-aggressive attempt to "say" things without saying them—and without incurring the consequences that would come if they were said out loud. At best, it is dishonest. Early on in the reconciliation process, this kind of communication is tempting and difficult to resist. Nevertheless, you must take the necessary steps to avoid it. Hiding recrimination and judgment behind a forced smile does nothing to alter its corrosive effect on the goal you set of rebuilding trust.

But this point is also about something much deeper than simply what happens in face-to-face communication with someone who has hurt you. It's about not allowing your own thoughts and feelings *to go on hurting you.* The real power of this advice has greatest effect when you are alone, when your mind wanders, and when your gut twists reflexively at the memory of what has happened.

The truth is, the actual act of betrayal is over and done with. If it weren't, you wouldn't now be working toward rebuilding trust. The offense no longer exists anywhere but in the past. But that is exactly where your mind likes to spend its time, endlessly reliving painful moments, rehearsing what you should have said or done differently, and embellishing things with imaginative details that frequently aren't true. All of this, in turn, serves to keep your wounds fresh and your feelings raw. Dwelling on the past is to reconciliation as Kryptonite is to Superman— toxic. Every step in this list urges you to do exactly the opposite, to be in the present moment where both of you have committed to healing what's broken.

> "WHATEVER IS TRUE,
> WHATEVER IS NOBLE,
> WHATEVER IS RIGHT,
> WHATEVER IS PURE,
> WHATEVER IS LOVELY,
> WHATEVER IS ADMIRABLE—
> IF ANYTHING IS EXCELLENT
> OR PRAISEWORTHY—THINK
> ABOUT SUCH THINGS."
>
> —Philippians 4:8

"Guarding" your thoughts and feelings means taking charge of them and interrupting the mind's natural propensity for obsessive stewing. Here are three simple tips for how to do that:

Breathe.

On one hand, this advice is highly practical and beneficial to your immediate health. Anxiety that's fueled by fear and anger has all sorts of negative effects on our physical wellbeing. An article published by the Harvard Medical School states that "anxiety prepares us to confront a crisis by putting the body on alert. But its physical effects can be counterproductive, causing light-headedness, nausea, diarrhea, and frequent urination. And when it persists, anxiety can take a toll on our mental and physical health."[3] And that's before you consider how anxiety can disrupt healthy eating and sleep habits, and inhibit proper exercise. Furthermore, anxiety has been linked to a number of other disorders, including heart disease, migraine headaches, insomnia, chronic respiratory disorders and gastrointestinal disorders. Untreated anxiety often makes dealing with associated physical conditions much more difficult.

Letting your mind endlessly chew on painful memories is a recipe for crippling anxiety. Consciously taking at least three deep breathes in a row is a proven technique for releasing that tension. Beyond that, mindful breathing is an ancient practice aimed at calming the mind and centering your thoughts where you want them to be, not where they reflexively run.

Be present.

Is there a place your thoughts can be where the pain of betrayal is not still fresh? Yes! Here and now. Your breathing opens the door for the mind to experience this moment, exactly as it is. To center yourself in the present, pay attention to your senses—to sounds, sensations, sights, and smells that you were oblivious to while ruminating in the past. Let those signals be the sole focus of attention, and watch the calming effect this has on you.

Be thankful.

Gratitude is powerful medicine—even in its smallest expression. You don't have to force a prayer of thanks you may or may not genuinely feel for big picture things. Pick something in your surroundings and say thank you. For sunshine on the carpet, the sound of hummingbirds at the feeder outside, the smell of dinner cooking.

LETTING YOUR MIND ENDLESSLY CHEW ON PAINFUL MEMORIES IS A RECIPE FOR CRIPPLING ANXIETY.

One final word on this point about guarding your words: beware the dangers of gossip. A painful betrayal can also make for a dramatic *story*. It is natural to share what's happening in your life with people close to you. But be careful that keeping them informed doesn't become an excuse to relive the event over and over, or as license to verbally trash the one who hurt you to others. Instead, use your words to reinforce your belief that reconciliation and healing are possible.

STEP 6 **Define Your Boundaries.**

Neil Clark Warren—author, psychologist, and founder of the online dating giant eHarmony—encouraged people looking for lasting romance to take a hard look at their deepest desires before ever going on a first date. He coached them to develop a list of their personal "must-haves" and "can't-stands"—a relationship manifesto to guide their search. These items represented the non-negotiable things they wanted (or didn't want) in a partner. Dr. Warren believed most people had only a vague idea of what they were looking for. Armed with specifics, he reasoned, it's easier to recognize when someone is not right before you invest months or years in the relationship.[4]

Rebuilding trust after a betrayal is also an excellent time to put this technique to work. In this case, it's not about assessing whether the relationship is right for you; you've already decided it is. Rather, this can set concrete boundaries to help you put a relationship that has fallen out of balance back into alignment with your values and desires. It's not very helpful for you to say to someone, "Be what I want." The person need to know exactly what that means—which means you must know, in detail.

In many respects, this step overlaps with step three in this list: consider your role in what has occurred. Why? Because it's common to discover that your existing boundaries have been out of whack in unhelpful ways. This takes one of two paths:

- **You had no boundaries.** In everyday life, you let things go in order to get along, and in so doing, helped create the perception that you were okay with anything. This doesn't mean the eventual betrayal was your fault! But seeing this for what it is will help you know what must happen going forward.

- **Your boundaries were too rigid.** Defining your "must-haves" and "can't-stands" at this point in the process can help you see if your expectations are set too high. For example, a woman who demands that her husband never—under any circumstances—have a friendly conversation with another female is setting unrealistic traps for him and herself. She is likely to see betrayal where none exists and to put her partner on the defensive unnecessarily.

To know what you want—and where you have been on the boundaries spectrum—takes concerted introspection. Writing for *Psychology Today*, Dr. Abigail Brenner put it like this:

> Get to know yourself as best you can. This means that you need to learn what's really important to you, what you really value apart from anyone else. Gaining access to your inner world by becoming familiar and comfortable with your own beliefs, emotions, feelings, and ideas is essential.[5]

Spend time discovering these things about yourself, so you can move on to the next step.

STEP 7 Communicate Your Boundaries.

Knowing your limits is great, but only if you can effectively let others know as well. It is surprisingly difficult for many people to verbalize what they want and need. Here are some tips for making that easier.

Write it down.

Part of the problem with tough conversations is that few of us are skilled at thinking on our feet. It all sounds great in our heads, but as soon as we start speaking, the words get tangled. One unexpected question from the other person is enough to derail the train entirely. Making a list of talking points in advance, when you can choose your words carefully and be precise with what you mean, will help keep your feet under you.

Choose the right time.

If either of you is tired, rushed, or stressed by other things, that's not the right time. Do what you must to be sure you are both at your best.

Set the stage.

Difficult discussions sometimes get off on the wrong foot because the other person feels taken off guard.

Avoid this by scheduling a time to talk and letting him know in advance what you want to discuss. This communicates that you consider the conversation to be much more than casual—and gives him the chance to mentally prepare.

Stay calm.

If you've done the work of defining your boundaries in the previous step, then there is nothing for you to defend or justify. You are simply stating what is true for you, with no need for anyone else's approval or consent. With this in mind, you will be able to keep your cool if the other person grows tense.

If you pay attention to these fundamentals, then this vital conversation can become a template for better communication about all kinds of things as you rebuild your relationship.

PREPARING TO COMMUNICATE
YOUR BOUNDARIES

Write it down.

What will I say? (Be specific.)

_____

_____

_____

_____

Choose the right time.

When would be the best time and what would be the best location for me and _____ [person's name] to have this conversation?

_____

_____

_____

_____

Set the stage.

When and where is this conversation scheduled to take place?

_____

_____

_____

_____

_____

Stay calm.

If I start feeling tense or angry, what will I do or remind myself of so that I remain calm?

_____

_____

_____

_____

_____

STEP 8 Hold Your Boundaries.

You know what you want and need. You've let the other person know as well. Now comes the really tricky part: making sure those boundaries are respected and enforced. Recall the building officials who set new standards in response to disaster? Making sure those rules are followed is key to preventing future harm.

How to do that is remarkably simple, but not necessarily easy. Here's how:

Be consistent.

Once you've communicated your boundaries, then it's up to you to avoid letting things slide. Mixed messages will undermine everything you've worked for so far.

Be firm.

People often fail to consistently enforce their own boundaries because they fail to understand the difference between assertiveness and aggression. We fear appearing pushy or combative. But clear, direct communication is perfectly reasonable behavior and necessary when it comes to holding your ground.

Be grateful.

Don't be afraid to acknowledge when someone succeeds in changing their behavior to accommodate your boundaries.

STEP 9 **Honor the Other Person's Boundaries.**

Once again, just because you are the one who suffered the betrayal does not mean these rules do not apply to you as well. Communicating your boundaries is likely to elicit a desire in the other person to do likewise. Treat them with the same respect you want for yourself.

STEP 10   Regularly Assess Your Progress.

You've come a long way and worked hard to lay a solid foundation for rebuilding trust. But as I said earlier, there is no autopilot setting. It remains necessary for some time to monitor the process for red flags and signs that you have begun to drift off course.

Check in with yourself:

- How strong is your level of commitment to reconciliation?

- Where in your life are you doing the work of forgiveness?

- Have you corrected aspects of your behavior that may have contributed to what happened?

- Where are your thoughts, feelings, and words?

- Do your boundaries need further refinement?

- Have you been consistent in enforcing your boundaries?

- Are you respecting the other person's boundaries as well?

Check in with the other person:

- Are accountability measures in place and working?

- Is the person struggling to correct his/her behavior and needs help?

- What is his/her level of commitment to reconciliation?

Don't be surprised by setbacks. They happen, and frequent check-ins are the way to deal with them before they spin out of control. But never lose sight of the truth that reconciliation is possible—and likely—when both of you are willing to invest the work.

Psychologist Randi Gunther, PhD, describes that potential beautifully:

> If love and other sacred attachments are still present, those betrayed partners must be open to examine their own participation in what has happened and work hard to get through the understandable need to express their wounds and desires to retaliate. When the couples I've known who have been fully willing to commit to this hazardous journey, they look back at the betrayal as the wake-up call that preceded a new level of commitment and depth in their relationship.[6]

In other words, doing the work described above will be hard, but it holds the potential to do more than help you "get over" the betrayal. On the other side, your relationship can be stronger than ever!

What *to* Do When You Did *the* Betraying

After confessing to Gary what she had done to harm their finances and betray his trust, Rita was consumed by overwhelming guilt. She lost all confidence in herself and entered a period of depression characterized by intense self-loathing. The ground heaved beneath her feet as well. Like Gary, Rita doubted the future viability of her marriage—but from the opposite direction. She questioned her own fitness to be a good partner for Gary, given her devious actions.

NEVER LOSE SIGHT OF THE TRUTH THAT RECONCILIATION IS POSSIBLE—AND LIKELY—WHEN BOTH OF YOU ARE WILLING TO INVEST THE WORK.

Rita fell prey to the same fallacy that haunts many people who have betrayed the trust of someone they care about: She equated what she had done with *who she was as a person*. She believed her poor decision-making was evidence that she was a hopelessly flawed human.

"How can I expect him to ever trust me again?" she asked me.

In essence, Rita agreed with Gary's initial position that what she had done was "unforgivable." This is why we start this list of steps with the essential component described in the previous list.

STEP 1 Forgive ... *Yourself.*

The truth is, people who feel no remorse and see no need to forgive themselves typically do not inspire in others a desire for reconciliation in the first place. More often, the ones who did the betraying are appalled at their actions and need to be reminded that mistakes are only that—mistakes. We all make them from time to time, and our missteps can nearly always be corrected.

This is anything but easy, however. In fact, forgiving yourself can be much harder to do than forgiving someone else.

> Forgiveness is often defined as a deliberate decision to let go of feelings of anger, resentment, and retribution toward someone who you believe has wronged you. However, while you may be quite

generous in your ability to forgive others, you may be much harder on yourself. Everyone makes mistakes, but learning how to learn from these errors, let go, move on, and forgive yourself is important for mental health and well-being.[7]

In my experience, a powerful first step is to *accept* what you have done. We all secretly harbor the idea that we are above bad decisions and mistaken behavior.

"What was I thinking?" Rita said. "How could I be so stupid?"

"Do you really expect to find answers to that?" I asked.

"No, not really."

"Good," I said. "Then you're free to just let it be what it is and move on to what happens next."

Until you can do that, you're likely to be stuck, unable to tackle everything else on this list.

STEP 2 Be Honest.

Once you've accepted in broad strokes that, for whatever reason, you made choices that led you to betray someone you care about, now it's time to come clean with transparency and vulnerability. A common mistake—and a real obstacle to genuine reconciliation—is for the one who committed the offense to downplay the severity of their actions or even hide some of the unflattering particulars. To succeed at rebuilding trust, *everything* must be known and in the open. Anything less is just another lie and a reason for the other person to feel doubly betrayed, if and when the truth emerges.

When this hard conversation happens, imagine yourself in a court of law. See yourself taking the stand having just sworn "to tell the truth, the whole truth, and nothing but the truth." Leave nothing out.

STEP 3 Be Sorry ... *Genuinely.*

A tough question the one who was betrayed is likely to ask is this: "Are you truly sorry you did this to me—or only sorry the truth came out?" It's a legitimate fear. While it's impossible for you to offer conclusive proof one way or another, here are things you can do to give compelling evidence of the former. Not only will this reassure the person you offended, it is a handy litmus test for you as well. If you find it difficult to do any of the following, more self-reflection is in order.

Be specific.

Vagueness is the hallmark of a person with something to hide. Don't just say, "I'm sorry." Make sure the person knows *you* know exactly what you have to be sorry for. For instance, during her process of reconciliation with Gary, Rita learned to say, "I'm sorry that I put your dream of owning a home at risk by breaking our agreement."

Show, don't just tell.

In the early days of working toward reconciliation, chances are your words will count for very little. Actions speak much louder anyway, and they can't be denied. Demonstrate your remorse in all the everyday things you now do differently, better, and more thoughtfully. This is not about buying your way back into favor. It's about genuine gift-giving as a way to say, "I'm sorry for the past, and I care about our future."

Hold yourself accountable.

Someone who is truly sorry will not make the one they've harmed monitor and enforce agreed upon accountability measures. Do it yourself. Go above and beyond.

Never make excuses or try to shift blame.

Just don't. You did what you did, period.

STEP 4   Don't Push.

It should be abundantly obvious by now that trust is extremely fragile. Once damaged, it will not grow back quickly. As the one who did the betraying, it's not for you to say where the benchmarks are or when they should be reached. Trying to rush the one you harmed into steps they are not yet ready to take is a sure way to cast doubt on your long-haul commitment and undo any progress you've made.

STEP 5   Accept Appropriate Accountability.

As part of their reconciliation plan, Gary and Rita agreed that he would take over the management of her personal checking account for a period of time to give him confidence that there were no more hidden expenses.

"I'd been taking care of my own finances since I turned sixteen," Rita said. "So, yes, this was hard to do."

But she understood it was a reasonable request and readily agreed to it for the sake of healing what she had broken. Make sure you are willing to do the same.

STEP 6 Accept Forgiveness.

Sometimes the moment comes when the betrayed one is ready to take steps to restore the relationship to its previous footing of trust, but is stopped short because the one who betrayed them is unable to receive what's being offered. If all your hard work of healing is poised to pay off, let it!

When Jesus healed a paralyzed man, he sent him away with the words, "Your sins are forgiven" (Matthew 9:1–8; see also Luke 7:36–50). That is the prize you've sought, so don't be afraid to receive it when the time comes.

STEP 7 Make Healing Changes Last.

To a woman caught in adultery, Jesus said, "Go now and leave your life of sin" (John 8:2–11). As reconciliation grows into a restored, renewed, and resurgent relationship, guard against old habits of thought and behavior. As the apostle Paul wrote, "Therefore, if anyone is in Christ, the new creation has come: The old has gone, the new is here! All this is from God, who reconciled us to himself through Christ and gave us the ministry of reconciliation" (2 Corinthians 5:17–18).

What *to* Do Together

Finally, let's consider a vital dimension of rebuilding trust—one that too many people overlook. This is where you knit together the work you do as individuals into a renewed and strengthened relationship. Working together is not just about making time for all those "check-ins" and for monitoring accountability measures. It's about truly seeing each other with fresh eyes and letting all these steps become more than the sum of the parts. Here's how.

STEP 1 Listen!

It's no secret that we live in a deafening world. News media, social media, entertainment media, marketing media—all clamor for attention without ceasing. Add to that the demands of bosses, coworkers, friends, kids, and extended family, and you've got a perfect storm of distraction.

If Richard Bach is right and this crisis of betrayal has a gift for you in its hands, then maybe it is this: doing the work of forgiveness, healing, and reconciliation forces you to hear each other in ways that probably haven't existed for you in a long time, if ever. To do this right, you'll put down the phone, turn the TV off, tell others you can't be disturbed, and then focus on each other.

Here's the crux of this advice: When you've done that, listen to each other like never before. Really *listen*, and be prepared to hear what you've missed or ignored or denied. This is the magic carpet with the power to lift you above your pain and into the relationship you were meant to have.

STEP 2 Set Mutual Goals.

Much of what I've shared so far has focused on what's needed for you as an individual. I've challenged you to understand:

- What is my role?

- What are my boundaries?

- What do I want and need?

- What must I take responsibility for?

All of that is profitable and necessary. It provides a firm foundation so you can now turn to asking:

- What do *we* want?

FORGIVENESS, HEALING, AND RECONCILIATION FORCES YOU TO HEAR EACH OTHER IN WAYS THAT PROBABLY HAVEN'T EXISTED FOR YOU IN A LONG TIME.

When Gary and Rita did this work, it became clear that in addition to a home of their own, they wanted to enjoy daily life along the way. They agreed that meant spending some of their income on little luxuries. The goal they set together was to have both.

Taking responsibility and improving yourself is the path that leads to a better life together.

STEP 3 Keep Forgiving.

Forgiveness is not a switch you flip and then never think about again. It is a choice you must keep making, not just regarding things in the past, but for all the new things that inevitably crop up along the way. I pray those are not of the same magnitude as the betrayal you face now. Even so, daily life is ripe with potential for small offenses that can grow into big divides if we let them.

FORGIVENESS IS A CHOICE YOU MUST KEEP MAKING.

This step belongs in the list of things you can do together to restore trust, because it involves creating a *culture of forgiveness* in your relationship. It means the mutual commitment to forgiveness as a way of life together.

STEP 4 Get Professional Help.

Last, but certainly not least, know when you need help and don't hesitate to find it. As I've said multiple times, nothing about this process is easy. The kind of self-reflection and painful communication you are called on to do can feel like quicksand pulling you under, and a therapist, pastor, or trusted counselor can provide a firm hand to keep you from sinking. Enlisting friends or family to help provide safe space can be effective, but the unbiased perspective of someone professionally trained to help you look at every angle is the preferred choice for many people.

> "WHAT, THEN, SHALL WE SAY IN RESPONSE TO THESE THINGS? IF GOD IS FOR US, WHO CAN BE AGAINST US? HE WHO DID NOT SPARE HIS OWN SON, BUT GAVE HIM UP FOR US ALL—HOW WILL HE NOT ALSO, ALONG WITH HIM, GRACIOUSLY GIVE US ALL THINGS?"
>
> —Romans 8:31-32

Hope *in* Healing

If I could choose one thing for you to take away from all this advice, it would be this: Betrayal—as painful as it is—need not be the end of your relationship. Earthquakes happen, but the same healing grace that knits broken bones and restores us to strength after illness is well able to reconcile your wounded hearts and renew your love for each other. Trust God to guide you through the work of rebuilding trust and you will emerge on the other side, better than ever. Meditate every day on what Paul wrote: "What, then, shall we say in response to these things? If God is for us, who can be against us" (Romans 8:31)?

BETRAYAL—AS PAINFUL AS IT IS—NEED NOT BE THE END OF YOUR RELATIONSHIP.

TWELVE WAYS TO RELEASE REGRET

Few people arrive at adulthood without regrets. You might have a handful of regrets or a bucketful. Regrets can keep you stuck, rob you of joy, and negatively affect your relationships moving forward.

When you experience an act of betrayal—whether you committed the act or suffered the consequences of another person's offense—you will likely have feelings of remorse and regret. But that doesn't mean you need to be burdened by them throughout your life. You can work through your regrets and release them so you can live with freedom and joy. Begin by pondering these twelve ways to let go of regret:

1. **Resolve not to live in the past.**
   Regrets keep us stuck in the past as we lament failures and missed opportunities. We ruminate about what might have been. We miss out on the joy of living today when we're haunted by the failures of yesterday.

2. **Don't deny your mistakes.**
   Denying past mistakes is like pretending you don't have a broken arm: you may learn to live with the pain, but it'll never set properly and will, in fact, cause more trouble over the long haul.

3. **Don't dwell on them either.**
   Dwelling on mistakes is like putting them under a microscope, which distorts reality and makes everything seem bigger than it really is.

4. **Forgive yourself.**

   Recognize that regret is a form of unforgiveness . . . *of yourself*. It may be easier to forgive others than yourself. But releasing yourself from guilt and shame is a key to moving beyond regret.

5. **Strive for self-acceptance.**

   You have made mistakes, maybe bad ones, but that doesn't mean you're defined by those blunders. Accept that you're human and that it does no good to relive your mistake over and over.

6. **Realize you're not alone.**

   Every person is somewhere on his or her own journey of figuring out how to deal with the what-ifs that are an inescapable part of life.

7. **Make your thoughts work for you.**

   Your self-talk—the voice you hear in your head throughout the day—is a powerful force. Purposefully replace your negative thoughts with positive ones.

8. **Understand the toxicity of regret.**

   Numerous scientific studies have shown that stressful thoughts and emotions can trigger disease-causing processes in our bodies. Carrying around regrets not only weighs on your psyche, but also erodes your physical health.

9. **Realize that regret robs you of positive energy.**
   Wrestling with pain and anger every day takes a lot of precious energy. It costs you lost sleep, robs you of peace and laughter, and taxes your muscles with constant tension.

10. **Identify lessons learned.**
    Nearly every experience—difficult or delightful—teaches us something. What insights can you discern that will enable you to avoid trouble next time around?

> "FOR [THE LORD'S] ANGER LASTS ONLY A MOMENT, BUT HIS FAVOR LASTS A LIFETIME; WEEPING MAY STAY FOR THE NIGHT, BUT REJOICING COMES IN THE MORNING."
>
> —Psalm 30:5

11. **Resolve to resolve it.**
    Regrets don't go away on their own. The healing process requires purposeful attention and action. There's no need to be weighed down any longer. Take steps to achieve inner peace.

12. **Make sure the slate is clean.**
    Regrets have a way of rearing their ugly heads even after you thought you'd put them down for good. Once you've taken steps to get beyond past mistakes and their repercussions, leave them behind. Don't let regrets regain ground in your life. Move on with a fresh start.

Emotional Equilibrium During Life's Seismic Shifts

As you seek to regain your footing after the earthquake of betrayal, it is vital to find emotional equilibrium. Counterbalance anger, fear, and guilt with optimism, hope, and joy. The promise of the whole-person approach means that the health aspects of a person can support the weaker characteristics until the whole person is strong and well. Intellectual, relational, physical, and spiritual aspects of your life can also assist you in sustaining the life-affirming emotions of optimism, hope, and joy. The following exercises will acquaint you to whole-person principles.

Intellectual Support

To support emotional balance, be aware of the information you are feeding to your mind. Try reading a positive, uplifting book, and *intentionally* set aside time in your day to fill yourself up intellectually with constructive, encouraging messages. Be aware of what you are reading and listening to, and seek to counter the negative input that we all get as a part of our day with positive influences.

Relational Support

Think of a person you really enjoy talking to, someone who makes you feel good about yourself or someone who's just fun to be around. It could be a family member, a coworker, a teller at the bank, or anyone who brings a smile to your day. *Intentionally* plan this week to spend time with that person, even if it's just for a moment or two. Make the effort to verbalize your appreciation for his or her positive presence in your day.

Physical Support

Physical activity is a wonderful way of promoting emotional health. Engage in some mild exercise this week. Take a walk around the neighborhood. Stroll through a city park. The goal is twofold: to get your body moving, and to allow you to focus on something other than yourself and your surroundings. Take a little time when you're at the park and watch someone playing with his dog, or cheer at a Little League game. *Intentionally* open up your focus to include the broader world around you.

YOU HAVE A *CHOICE*. TODAY, CHOOSE OPTIMISM, HOPE, AND JOY.

Spiritual Support

Take some time to nourish your spirit. If you are part of a church, make sure to attend services this week. If you are not, listen to some

spiritual or meditative music. Spend time in quiet reflection, meditation, or prayer. *Intentionally* engage in an activity that replenishes and reconnects your spirit.

■ ■ ■

Each of these actions may seem like a small step. They may not even seem achievable, given the way you feel. Please do them anyway. If you are emotionally out of sync, you can't rely on how you're feeling to determine what you do.

Each of these actions, done intentionally, will help you in two ways:

- They will assist you in focusing on optimism, hope, and joy.

- They will reinforce the truth that you can intentionally respond to life and its circumstances.

You have a *choice*. Today, choose optimism, hope, and joy.

Notes

1   Steven Stosny, "Life After Betrayal: Getting Past the Victim Identity," *Psychotherapy Network* (July/August 2013).

2   Richard Bach, *Illusions: The Adventures of a Reluctant Messiah* (1977).

3   "Anxiety and physical illness," *Harvard Health Publishing, Harvard Women's Health Watch* (July 2008; updated May 9, 2018).

4   These concepts are developed in Neil Clark Warren's books *Date or Soul Mate?* (Thomas Nelson, 2002) and *Falling in Love for All the Right Reasons* (Center Street, 2005).

5   Abigail Brenner, "7 tips to Create Healthy Boundaries with Others," *Psychology Today* (November 21, 2015).

6   Randi Gunther, "Can a Relationship Survive After Betrayal?" *Psychology Today* (September 30, 2016).

7   Kendra Cherry, "Taking the Steps to Forgive Yourself," *Verywell Mind: www.verywellmind.com* (June 29, 2020).

Image Credits

MORE RESOURCES FROM
DR. GREGORY L. JANTZ

Unmasking Emotional Abuse

Six Steps to Reduce Stress

Ten Tips for Parenting
the Smartphone Generation

Five Keys to Dealing
with Depression

Seven Answers for Anxiety

Five Keys to Raising Boys

Five Keys to Health
and Healing

40 Answers for
Teens' Top Questions

When a Loved One Is Addicted

Social Media and Depression

Rebuilding Trust after Betrayal

How to Deal with Toxic People

www.hendricksonrose.com